Taxing Consumption in a Global Economy

Harry Grubert and
T. Scott Newlon

The AEI Press

Publisher for the American Enterprise Institute
WASHINGTON, D.C.

1997

This study borrows extensively from Grubert and Newlon (1995). For comments on that paper, we thank Jay Mackie, Sheena McConnell, Barbara Rollinson, Joel Slemrod, Eric Toder, and Joann Weiner. Any views expressed here are those of the authors alone and should not be construed as reflecting the views or policies of the U.S. Treasury Department.

Available in the United States from the AEI Press, c/o Publisher Resources Inc., 1224 Heil Quaker Blvd., P.O. Box 7001, La Vergne, TN 37086-7001. Distributed outside the United States by arrangement with Eurospan, 3 Henrietta Street, London WC2E 8LU England.

ISBN 0-8447-7069-8

1 3 5 7 9 10 8 6 4 2

THE AEI PRESS
Publisher for the American Enterprise Institute
1150 17th Street, N.W., Washington, D.C. 20036

Printed in the United States of America

Contents

Foreword

Economists, policy makers, and business executives are keenly interested in fundamental tax reform. High marginal tax rates, complex tax provisions, disincentives for saving and investment, and solvency problems in the social security program provide reasons to contemplate how reforms of the tax code and other public policies toward saving and investment might increase economic efficiency, simplify the tax code, and enhance fairness. Many economists believe that gains to the economy from an overhaul of the income tax or from a move to a broad-based consumption tax can be measured in the trillions of dollars. Most conventional economic models indicate a potential for large gains from tax reform.

While many economists agree broadly on the simple analytics of tax reform, they are in much less agreement on such key empirical questions as how much saving or investment would rise in response to a switch to a consumption tax, how much capital accumulation would increase under a partial privatization of social security, how reform would affect the distribution of taxes, and how international capital markets influence the effects of tax reforms in the United States. This lack of professional consensus has made the policy debate fuzzy and confusing.

With these concerns in mind, Diana Furchtgott-Roth and I organized a tax reform seminar series at the American Enterprise Institute beginning in January 1996. At each seminar, an economist presented new empirical research on topics relating to fundamental tax reform. These topics include transition problems in moving to a consumption tax, the effect of taxation on household saving, distributional effects of consumption taxes in the long and short run, issues in the taxation of financial services, privatizing social security as a fundamental tax reform, international issues in consumption taxation, distributional consequences of reductions in the capital gains tax, effects of tax reform on pension saving and nonpension saving, effects of tax reform on labor supply, consequences of tax reform on business investment, and likely prototypes for fundamental tax reform.

The goal of the pamphlet series in fundamental tax reform is to distribute research on economic issues in tax reform to a broad audience. Each study in the series reflects many insightful comments by seminar participants— economists, attorneys, accountants, and journalists in the tax policy community. Diana and I are especially grateful to the two discussants of each paper, who offered the perspectives of an economist and an attorney.

I would like to thank the American Enterprise Institute for providing financial support for the seminar series and pamphlet series.

R. GLENN HUBBARD
Columbia University

1

Introduction

A number of recent tax reform proposals would replace the U.S. income tax system with one based on consumption. Much ink has been spilled in analyzing the effects of such a change on incentives, distributional considerations, and compliance burdens, but the analysis is often placed in a closed-economy context. Our purpose in this volume is to lay out issues that arise from the fact that the United States has an open economy, with cross-border flows of capital, technology, and trade. Open-economy considerations raise new issues and can alter results implied by a closed-economy analysis.

Several variants on a consumption tax have been proposed, including the so-called flat tax, the unlimited savings allowance (USA) tax, a value-added tax (VAT), and a retail sales tax. A flat tax proposal modeled on the plan developed by Hall and Rabushka (1995) has been put forward by House Majority Leader Richard Armey. Under the flat tax scheme, individuals are taxed only on their wage income (including pensions), and businesses are taxed on their cash flow measured as sales less purchases, including capital purchases and wages. The USA tax, proposed by Senators Sam Nunn and Pete Domenici, actually consists of two separate consumption taxes. At the individual level, the USA tax imposes a consumed-income tax, that is, a tax on income less savings (plus dissavings).

At the business level, the USA tax imposes a subtraction-method VAT; that is, tax is paid on sales less purchases, where purchases include capital purchases but not wages. Various VAT plans have been proposed, perhaps most notably the detailed plan offered by Representative Sam Gibbons. Support for a federal retail sales tax has been expressed by, among others, Representative Bill Archer, chairman of the House Ways and Means Committee, and Senator Richard Lugar.

For our purposes, it is generally not necessary to go into many of the specific details of these plans. Most of the international issues we present can be illustrated in the context of two generic types of flat rate consumption taxes, which differ only in the treatment of exports and imports. The first is a destination-basis consumption tax, in which exports are exempt from tax and imports are taxed (that is, there are border tax adjustments). The USA business tax (and most VATs), a consumed-income tax, and a retail sales tax are all examples of consumption taxes that are imposed on a destination basis. The second is an origin-basis consumption tax, in which exports are taxed and imports are exempt (that is, there are no border tax adjustments). The flat tax is an example of an origin-basis consumption tax. We will discuss the significance of this distinction below. In many places the discussion focuses on the business components of the consumption tax proposals.

The next chapter of this volume summarizes key features of the proposals important to the analysis. The following chapters analyze the implications of the plans for the activities of multinational companies (MNCs), international capital flows and trade, tax avoidance opportunities, and the complexity of international tax provisions, transition incidence, and the reactions of other countries. The last chapter presents some conclusions.

2
Key Features of the Plans

The Tax Base

All the proposals considered here have consumption bases. The flat tax and USA business tax, for example, are essentially both subtraction-method VATs in that purchases of goods and services are immediately deductible, including capital expenditures. The flat tax differs from the typical consumption VAT only in that wages are deductible at the business level and taxable at the personal level. The USA individual tax is a consumed-income tax in that the consumption base is arrived at by deducting from (including in) income a measure of net new saving (dissaving).

The principal significance of the consumption base is that an investment in the United States earns the pretax rate of return to capital. For a tax rate of t, a dollar's worth of capital can be bought with $1-t$ dollars because it is immediately deductible (that is, it is expensed), and each year the investment will pay $1-t$ of its cash flow after tax. The expensing of the capital invested and taxation of the cash flow occur at the business level under a flat tax or subtraction-method VAT and at the individual level under a consumed-income tax. Because the present value of the cash flow from a dollar invested at the margin should be equal to a dollar, the value of the expensing is just equal

3

to the present value of the tax on the future cash flow from a dollar invested at the margin, and there is no tax on the return to new capital at the margin. There is tax on inframarginal, above-normal returns because the present value of the tax on the future cash flow will exceed the value of the initial deduction. An investment project that is worthwhile in the absence of the tax, however, will remain worthwhile with the tax, and the choice among investments would not be affected by the tax.

By contrast, under an ideal income tax, in which depreciation allowances match economic depreciation, marginal as well as inframarginal returns to capital would be taxed. Under such a tax, returns to capital would be taxed only once, either at the business level or at the individual level. The current U.S. tax system departs substantially from this ideal income VAT. There is a classical corporate income tax in which equity income is taxed once at the corporate level and then again when distributed at the personal level. Interest income is taxed, if at all, only at the personal level, since it is deductible at the business level. Depreciation allowances are not necessarily related to economic depreciation, and nominal, rather than real, interest is taxed. There are also substantial tax-favored sectors, including owner-occupied housing, tax-exempt entities such as pension funds, and the state and local government sector, which benefits from being able to issue tax-exempt bonds. And noncorporate business is also taxed more favorably than corporate business.

Given these complications, it cannot be presumed that much tax is paid on capital income. In fact, in an analysis of 1983 data, Gordon and Slemrod (1988) estimated that the United States collected very little revenue from the taxation of capital income. Even so, they did find that some revenue was collected, their results may have been partially attributable to cyclical effects, and the 1986 Tax Reform Act significantly narrowed the scope for the tax arbitrage that allowed capital income to escape tax or, in fact, to be tax favored.[1] Consequently, we shall assume that the current U.S. tax system does impose some tax on capital income; however, the complications we have outlined above will prove important in analyzing the effects of the proposals on capital flows.

Real versus Financial Transactions

The flat tax, the USA business tax, and consumption VATs in general use what is called an R base (for real, as distinct from financial, transactions), a terminology used in the 1978 Meade committee report.[2] Under an R-based tax, sales of goods and services are taxed, and purchases of goods and services are deductible; but financial transactions, including the payment and receipt of interest and dividends, are ignored. This arrangement creates an issue, familiar to those who have studied the VAT, concerning the taxation of banks and other financial intermediaries.[3] In the context of this volume, one implication is that while interest is not deductible from the U.S. tax base, it will still be deductible in countries that retain an income tax.

The USA individual tax is an example of an $(R+F)$-based tax, in which real and financial transactions enter the tax base. Under an $(R+F)$ base, net increases (decreases) in financial assets are taxable (deductible). In the context of debt, then, cash receipts from borrowing (a borrower's proceeds from the issuance of new debt or a lender's receipts of interest or principal repayments) are taxable, and cash payments from borrowing (a borrower's interest payments and repayments of principal or a lender's new loans) are deductible. McLure and Zodrow (1995) have proposed a consumption tax system that is the reverse of the USA tax in that the business-level tax is on an $(R+F)$ base, while the personal-level tax is on an R base.[4]

Nondeductibility of Interest

Under the flat tax, the USA business tax, and all VATs, interest expense is not deductible at the business level, and interest income is not taxed. In a purely domestic context, this change is innocuous to the extent that the elimination of interest deductibility is compensated for by the elimination of tax on interest income. But the increase in tax from the loss in interest deductions may actually far exceed the tax saving from exemption of interest income, because so much interest income is not taxed under current law. Consequently, such a change would substantially increase the tax burden on debt-financed business investment. In an open economy, the shift to interest nondeductibility becomes even more significant because foreigners are already exempt from U.S. tax on portfolio interest. Because they derive no benefit from any personal-level exemption, foreigners would reduce their holdings of U.S. debt if the adoption of these proposals produced any tendency for U.S. interest rates to decline.

Treatment of Foreign Income

Under the current U.S. tax system, U.S.-resident individuals and businesses are subject to tax on their foreign income. In the case of income earned by foreign subsidiaries of U.S. multinational corporations, U.S. tax is generally not imposed until the income is distributed to the U.S. parent company as a dividend; this policy is known as deferral. At the time of income repatriation, a credit against U.S. tax liability is allowed for any foreign taxes paid directly on foreign income, for example, dividend withholding taxes. For dividend distributions from controlled foreign subsidiaries, U.S. MNCs also receive a foreign tax credit for underlying foreign corporation taxes on the income out of which the distribution is made. The foreign tax credit is limited to the amount of the U.S. tax liability on foreign income, so that any foreign tax in excess of that amount cannot be used to reduce other U.S. tax liabilities. Within limits imposed by separate "baskets" for different types of foreign income, excess foreign tax credits from one source of foreign income can be used to offset U.S. tax liability on other foreign income; this is sometimes called cross-crediting.

Under R-based consumption taxes such as the flat tax and the USA business tax, foreign interest and dividends, as well as the foreign earnings of U.S. MNCs, are exempt. Under $(R+F)$-based consumption taxes such as the USA individual tax, all interest and dividend receipts are taxed, but investment in both foreign and domestic assets is deductible, so that capital income is untaxed at the margin whether its source is foreign or domestic.

A business-level income tax could also exempt income from direct foreign investment, as is done in a number of other countries. Income from passive, or portfolio, foreign investment, however, could not realistically be exempted without leading to substantial erosion of the taxation of capital income.

Royalty receipts from foreign licensees are in a category distinct from interest and dividend income from foreign sources because they can be thought of as payments for the export of an intangible asset, just as lease payments from a foreign lessee to a lessor of U.S. machines are payments for the export of those machines. Under current tax law, receipts of royalties from abroad are included in foreign-source income, but, in principle, they could be included in domestic income under an income tax, as is income from the export of goods under current law generally.[5]

Based on this reasoning, the taxation of royalties should be consistent with the choice of destination or origin basis.[6] Royalty receipts from abroad should be exempt under the destination basis, and royalty payments to foreigners not deductible. Conversely, under the origin basis, all royalty receipts should be taxable and all royalty payments deductible.

Border Tax Adjustments

As we noted in the introduction, consumption taxes can be characterized as being either on a destination basis or on an origin basis, which describes the way imports and exports are treated. Under a destination-basis tax, exports are exempt from tax, and imports are taxed. Examples are the business component of the USA tax, a retail sales tax, and a cash flow consumed-income tax. Under an origin-basis tax, exports are taxed, and imports are exempt from tax. The flat tax is on an origin basis.

In some respects, a destination-basis tax is easiest to analyze because it is a pure consumption tax, and more specifically, it is a tax on consumption in the United States. Exports, which are not consumed in the United States, are exempt from tax; and imports, which are consumed in the United States, are taxed. From that feature, many implications flow. One, which is discussed later, is the irrelevance of the transfer-pricing issue, because ultimately only final consumption in the United States is in the tax base. An origin-basis tax has a somewhat more complicated base, U.S. consumption plus net exports, because aspects of U.S. production (that is, exports) are included in the base and aspects of consumption (that is, imports) are excluded. As we will see, in some respects the two bases are equivalent, and in other respects they are not.

It is commonly believed that the border tax adjustments under the destination-basis consumption tax, the exemption from tax of exports, and the tax on imports act as incentives for exports while discouraging imports. We will attempt to explain why this apparently common-sense view is incorrect. But we should be clear what we mean when we say that the border tax adjustments, by themselves, do not confer a trade advantage. It is not that a switch from an income tax, including the corporate tax, to a consumption tax, of any type, cannot affect trade.

The tax on business under the income tax can clearly

influence trade. The corporate income tax increases costs in the corporate sector (manufacturing, for example) relative to the noncorporate sector. Capital-intensive products are affected more than others. Accordingly, capital-intensive industries in the corporate sector will find their international competitiveness decline relative to more tax-favored sectors. A switch to a consumption tax, which does not tax capital on the margin, will obviously neutralize these tax-induced differences in costs.

Therefore, to focus on the consequences of the border tax adjustments alone, not the switch from an income tax, let us assume that a destination-basis consumption tax is enacted starting from a no-tax world. Alternatively, the new destination-basis consumption tax might be an "add-on" tax without other taxes being lowered.

Let us see how the decisions of consumers and producers are affected by the introduction of the destination-basis consumption tax. Are exporters any better situated than they were before the enactment of the tax? No, the exemption of exports will just get them to the position they were in before the consumption tax. The prices on exports they can offer are the same as before imposition of the consumption tax. Imposing a tax and then removing it does not leave them any better off in world markets.

What about the decisions of consumers? To them, the relative price of foreign goods and domestic goods has not changed. The destination-basis tax applies to all consumption, irrespective of where the goods were produced. U.S. consumers will, therefore, make the same choices between foreign and domestic goods as before the introduction of the tax. Accordingly, neither the prices of exports nor the U.S. demand for imports is affected by the destination-basis tax. No trade benefit is provided.

Now that we have seen that the enactment of a destination-basis consumption tax by itself is not an export incentive, we are in a better position to see whether switching from a destination-basis tax to an origin-basis tax makes a difference. Take an exporter who is considering selling one dollar more abroad. In real terms, the proceeds from those additional exports can be used for one of two purposes, to finance a dollar more of imports currently or to reinvest the dollar abroad. But if the dollar is invested abroad and the investment is at the margin, eventually it will finance imports with a present value of a dollar because a marginal investment should earn just a normal return. Accordingly, there is a simple equality between the value of the additional exports and the present value of the additional imports they will finance. That is,

increase in exports = present value of increase
in imports.

If we apply the tax rate t to both sides, we still have an equality,

t x increase in exports = t x present value of in
crease in imports.

On the left-hand side is the tax on the additional exports under the origin basis. On the right is the present value of the tax on the resulting additional imports under the destination basis. In present-value terms, the additional tax due to the increase in exports is identical under the two bases. Thus, the destination- and the origin-basis tax are equivalent for investment and trade decisions on the margin.

It is perhaps convenient to think of the origin-basis tax as a prepayment system compared with the destination-basis tax. The tax is prepaid on the exports going out. Eventually, a destination-basis tax collects an equivalent amount of tax on the imports financed by the additional exports.

The simple equality above for trade or investment with normal returns on the margin can be used to illustrate when the two bases are not equivalent. Consider, for example, the case in which U.S. investors have assets abroad before the consumption tax is enacted. In that case, under the origin-basis tax there is no tax on the consumption financed by the earnings on these assets abroad. There has been no prepayment of tax on the exports that financed the acquisition of these assets, and there is no tax on the imports coming in. But there is a tax under the destination basis because all U.S. consumption, including imports, is taxed. Thus, the destination and origin bases are not equivalent with respect to the initial cross-ownership of assets when the consumption tax is enacted.

Again, the origin and destination bases are not equivalent when the prospective investment abroad will earn above-normal returns. In that case, the tax on the additional exports that finance the foreign investment is less than the present value of the eventual imports made possible by the investment abroad. The origin-basis tax will, therefore, be less, in present-value terms, than the destination-basis tax. U.S. investors expecting to earn an above-normal return abroad would prefer the origin-basis tax. (This is related to the question of how royalties are taxed under the origin basis.)

The two bases are also not equivalent if a U.S. resident earns income in the United States and goes abroad to consume. In that case, there is no tax on the consumption abroad under the destination-basis tax because the consumption goods are not imported into the United States. In real terms, this consumption abroad will be financed by U.S. exports, which are not taxed under the destination basis, since U.S. tax on exports is rebated at the border. So going abroad to consume escapes the U.S. consumption tax if it is on a destination basis. (A consumed-income tax, such as the USA individual tax, is an exception to this conclusion if U.S. residents continue to be subject to the tax even if they consume abroad.)

But an origin-basis tax will tax the consumption abroad because it has to be financed by U.S. exports, which are taxed under the origin basis. Thus, under the origin-basis tax, U.S. taxpayers obtain tax-free consumption only if they have been fortunate enough to take their capital abroad before the introduction of the consumption tax. Under the destination-basis tax, they have an incentive to take themselves abroad to consume.

3

Effects on Multinational Business

Multinational companies account for a significant proportion of cross-border trade and investment flows. The effects of moving to a consumption tax on the incentives faced by MNCs are therefore of considerable significance. In this chapter, we consider how moving to a consumption tax system would affect the decisions of MNCs regarding the location of production, intangible assets, the performance of R&D, and the financial structure of the multinational group. In examining the MNC decision on investment location, we implicitly treat investments as being equity financed.[7]

Location of Production by U.S. MNCs

Under most consumption taxes (including the flat tax, the USA business tax, a retail sales tax, or a VAT), the foreign income of U.S. MNCs would be exempt from U.S. tax. The question arises whether this exemption would make investment in low-tax foreign jurisdictions relatively more attractive than it currently is. This is the so-called runaway plant problem, wherein production is shifted to low-tax foreign jurisdictions. Although exemption of foreign income from tax would lead to incentives for U.S. MNCs to locate tangible capital in low-tax jurisdictions if the United States retained an income tax, the case would not necessarily be the same if a consumption tax were substituted for the income tax. In fact, switching to a consumption tax would result in a greater preference by U.S. MNCs for investment in the United States, even in most cases as compared with investment in low-tax countries.

Under an income tax, the exemption of foreign income from tax would provide MNCs with an incentive to invest in low-tax jurisdictions, because the low foreign tax would be the final tax on the foreign income. If, in contrast, foreign income were taxed as it accrued, providing a credit for the foreign taxes paid on the income, there would be no tax motivation for domestically based MNCs to invest in low-tax foreign jurisdictions because the same rate of tax (the home country rate) would be paid wherever the investment was located. In reality, the current U.S. system for taxing foreign income provides incentives that are somewhere in between the pure exemption system and the taxation of foreign income on an accrual basis. Although the foreign income of a U.S. MNC is subject to U.S. tax, because the U.S. tax is often deferred until the income is repatriated to the United States (and because foreign taxes are credited against the U.S. tax liability on an overall basis, allowing cross-crediting from high- to low-tax items of foreign income), the incentives for investment in low-tax jurisdictions can sometimes approach, or even be the same as, those under an exemption system.[8]

The major effect on U.S. MNCs of replacing the income tax with a consumption tax may therefore result from the elimination of tax on normal returns to new investment in the United States. That should lower the tax on U.S. MNC investment in the United States relative to investment in all foreign locations, whether high or low tax.

There would be some difference on this score between a destination-basis and an origin-basis consumption tax. Under a destination-basis tax, U.S. MNCs would face the same U.S. tax (only on above-normal returns) whether they invested at home or abroad because foreign investment would implicitly receive the same treatment as domestic investment: the consumption financed by the return from the investment would be taxed. An equivalent investment abroad would cost less (because, viewed in real terms, there would be a rebate of tax on the exports necessary to finance the investment) by an amount equal to the value of expensing on the domestic investment, but the value of the return from the foreign investment would also be less by the amount of the tax.[9] Thus, the U.S. tax would be entirely neutral on the choice between domestic and foreign investment, and any foreign income tax, no matter how low the rate, would discourage foreign investment relative to U.S. investment.

Under an origin-basis tax, however, some incentive could remain for investment in low-tax foreign jurisdictions. Recall that in this case the exports that in real terms finance a foreign investment would be taxed but the stream of imports that represent the real return to the investment would not be taxed. Thus, for foreign investment there would be no implicit expensing but also no taxation of the return under an origin-basis consumption tax. For normal returns, the lack of expensing is exactly offset by the absence of tax on the return. But any above-normal returns on foreign investment escape tax under the origin basis.

The possibility of sheltering above-normal returns in a low-tax foreign jurisdiction might make that a relatively more attractive location for investment. The nature and significance of these location incentives under the origin basis may depend on the nature of the above-normal returns. Where above-normal returns reflect merely the outcome of risky investment, there might be no tax motivation to undertake that investment in a low-tax jurisdiction, since the expected benefit from lower taxes on favorable outcomes would presumably be offset by the expected loss from lower deductions for unfavorable outcomes. Where above-normal returns reflect economic rents—due to unique skills or know-how previously developed by the firm, for example—these rents should presumably be taxed in the location in which they were developed. This situation gives rise to transfer-pricing issues that are discussed further below.

Beyond the direct effects of replacing the income tax with a consumption tax, the location decisions of U.S. MNCs would also be affected by the elimination of the foreign tax credit. Because the tax cost of investing in foreign countries could no longer be offset by credits against U.S. taxes, U.S. MNCs would have a general incentive to lower their foreign tax burden by shifting investment out of high-tax foreign locations and into not only the United States but also low-tax foreign locations. As a result, U.S. MNCs could move their investments within Europe, for example, from high-tax countries such as Germany to low-tax countries such as Ireland and Switzerland.

Location of Production by Foreign MNCs

In the case of investment by a foreign MNC, its income from investment elsewhere is, of course, exempt from U.S. tax in any case, so the introduction of a consumption tax does not affect the after-tax return from alternatives to investment in the United States. Therefore, any reduction in tax on its returns to investment in the United States induced by moving to a consumption tax would make the United States a more attractive location for investment.

There is again some difference in the effects of destination- and origin-basis consumption taxes. Under an origin-basis consumption tax, investment by foreign MNCs would be treated identically to investment by domestic firms, so that U.S. tax would be paid only on above-normal returns. As discussed in relation to the effects on location decisions of U.S. multinationals, taxing above-normal returns could leave some incentive to invest in low-tax foreign jurisdictions instead of the United States, although that incentive would be reduced because normal investment returns would no longer be taxed. Under a destination-basis tax, however, foreign MNCs would pay no U.S. tax on normal or above-normal returns. In effect, the tax on above-normal returns paid by domestic investors is rebated at the border for foreign investors, since the exports that represent the real return from investment in the United States are relieved from tax.

The ultimate effects on the location incentives of foreign MNCs of moving to a consumption tax may vary depending on the tax rules of the home country. Where the home country exempts foreign income,[10] the U.S. tax (or lack thereof) is final, and reducing it by moving to a consumption tax would clearly make investment in the United States relatively more attractive. Where the home country taxes foreign income and provides a foreign tax credit,[11] the story is somewhat more complicated. To the extent that the reduction in U.S. tax on capital income results only in a reduction in the home country foreign tax credit, the United States is merely ceding tax revenue to the home country fisc without affecting the MNC's investment incentives. As discussed above, however, deferral and cross-crediting should enable many MNCs to keep a significant part of the benefit from a reduction in U.S. taxes on income capital.

An additional issue is whether countries that provide a credit for the current U.S. corporate income tax would also allow a credit for any portion of a consumption tax. Some countries that have considered a business cash-flow tax (as part of a consumption tax system) in place of a corporate income tax have been deterred by the perception that other countries might not provide a foreign tax credit for such taxes. Typically, countries that provide foreign tax credits do so either by domestic law or by tax treaty for taxes that look like corporate income taxes. Because the rationale for providing the credit is to preserve neutrality in the location of capital, the credit should apply to taxes imposed on capital income, such as a standard corporate income tax. Consumption taxes generally would not qualify simply because they are imposed on consumption and not on income.

There is, however, an argument for permitting a credit for a component of a consumption tax, but the argument applies only when the tax is imposed on an origin basis and there are above-normal returns. Even in that case, it depends on the origin of the above-normal returns.[12] For tangible investment with normal returns, an investment in the United States at the margin would not be affected by the provision of a home country credit because the initial reduction in credits when the investment is expensed, and U.S. tax is reduced, exactly offsets the value of the credits from the U.S. tax on the future returns from the investment. And, as explained previously, under a destination-basis consumption tax foreign investors would effectively bear no U.S. tax on normal or above-normal returns, so that no home country credit for U.S. taxes would be called for. But under an origin-basis consumption tax, investment in the United States would bear a tax on above-normal returns. In this case, the lack of a home country foreign tax credit for the U.S. tax on above-normal returns might discourage investment in the United States as compared with countries that imposed taxes that were creditable in the home country.

Too much significance should not be accorded the foreign tax credit issue. The lack of a foreign tax credit would create a disincentive to investment in the United States only to the extent that above-normal returns from the investment were not specific to the United States and could be earned if the MNC operated in other locations. Moreover, if the above-normal returns were attributable to intangible assets, then appropriate application of transfer-pricing rules would lead the above-normal returns to be taxed in the United States only if the intangible asset were created in the United States, and, consequently, the U.S. tax, and its creditability, would have no effect on the decision about where to exploit the intangible asset.[13]

Given the narrowness of the creditability issue, it seems likely that moving to a consumption tax would lead to increased investment in the United States by foreign MNCs whether or not other countries provided credits for any part of the U.S. tax.

Location of Intangible Assets

MNC decisions concerning where to exploit intangible assets such as patented processes and know-how will often be closely linked to their decisions regarding the location of their physical capital and production facilities. It is useful to consider in isolation the incentives affecting the location of intangible assets to highlight the issues specific to this location decision.

Under current law, U.S. companies with excess foreign tax credits have an incentive to exploit a U.S.-created intangible asset abroad because the royalty income that returns to the United States can escape both U.S. and foreign tax. This advantage occurs because the royalty payments are generally deductible in the foreign country, and, being classified under U.S. law as foreign-source income, excess foreign tax credits can be used to offset any U.S. tax liability on the royalty.

In contrast, a consumption tax, with appropriate treatment of royalties, would generally not influence the choice between exploiting an intangible asset at home and exploiting an intangible asset abroad. We would expect that, under a consumption tax, royalty receipts from abroad would be treated as payments for an export (of an intangible asset) and therefore would be exempt under the destination basis and taxed under the origin basis. The symmetric treatment of intangible (royalty) income from abroad and from domestic use is apparent under the origin basis: they face the same U.S. tax. The exemption of foreign royalty receipts under the destination basis, however, may create the appearance that foreign exploitation of intangible assets will avoid U.S. tax. This is not the case. The stream of returning royalties is effectively taxed under the destination basis as well, because in real terms the payment for the use of the intangible asset abroad is represented by a stream of imports, and those imports are taxed under the destination basis.

Thus, the consumption tax, whether it follows the origin or destination basis, does not distort the choice of location for exploiting the intangible asset if appropriate royalties are paid.[14] What if the appropriate royalty is not paid? Where there is imperfect enforcement of transfer-pricing rules, MNCs are able to set royalties that do not fully capture the value of an intangible asset transferred between members of the MNC group. The issue here is closely related to the one of above-normal returns discussed earlier, since above-normal returns apparently earned by an MNC in one country may actually be the result of an intangible asset created by the MNC in another country. The consequences are very different under the destination and the origin bases. Under the destination basis, since receipts of royalties from abroad do not enter into the MNC's tax base (and payments of royalties to foreigners are not deductible), the MNC gains no benefit from distorting royalty amounts to shift intangible income to the foreign location and loses to the extent that there is any foreign tax on that income. Under the origin basis, the MNC gains as long as the foreign tax rate is lower than the domestic tax rate. Thus, the possibility of tax avoidance through transfer-price manipulation may provide an incentive to locate intangible assets in low-tax foreign countries under an origin-basis tax but not under a destination-basis tax.

Location of R&D

MNCs can have some flexibility in determining the location of their investment in the creation of intangible capital through R&D.[15] Since these investment expenditures are currently expensed in the United States and most other countries, consumption tax treatment would not represent a direct change.[16] But current international tax rules have conflicting influences on the decision whether to locate R&D in the United States or abroad.

On the one hand, the R&D expense allocation rules often require U.S. companies to allocate a portion of U.S. R&D expense against foreign-source income. This allocation represents a partial disallowance of deductions for R&D expense for firms that have excess foreign tax credits, since the deduction is against foreign income that bears no U.S. tax in any case. Replacement of current rules with a consumption tax system would eliminate this disincentive to perform R&D in the United States.

On the other hand, as noted above, current tax rules also allow foreign-source royalty income to be shielded from any U.S. tax if the recipient company has excess foreign tax credits. This allowance creates an incentive for a U.S. company that expects to remain in an excess foreign tax credit position to undertake R&D in the United States.

A consumption tax would eliminate these conflicting incentives so that U.S. taxes would not distort the choice of location for R&D. Since the incentives conflict, it is not possible to say a priori what the net effect of their elimination would be on the level of R&D in the United States.

Location of Borrowing

Because under the consumption tax plans considered here interest expense would no longer be deductible in the United States, U.S. and foreign MNCs would have an incentive to shift debt to the books of their foreign affiliates to the extent that interest expense remained deductible in other countries.[17] The extent to which this would happen depends on the substitutability of borrowing by foreign affiliates for borrowing by a U.S. affiliate. There is some empirical evidence for such substitutability.[18] The revenue costs of such debt shifting would fall on foreign fiscs.

Transfer Pricing

The volume of transactions between the U.S. members of MNC groups and their foreign affiliates is large. These transactions include the sale of goods, the provision of services, the transfer of intangible assets, and lending. Under the current income tax, MNCs can have an incentive to distort the prices charged in those transactions to shift income from higher-tax jurisdictions to lower-tax jurisdictions. Income can be shifted out of the United States by lowering (raising) prices on goods, services, and intangible assets or by lowering (raising) interest rates on loans provided to (received from) affiliates in other tax jurisdictions.

Since interest is not deductible and not taxed under the consumption tax systems considered here, any incentive to shift income out of the United States by distorting interest charges on interaffiliate loans would be removed. There would, however, be an incentive to distort such interest charges to shift income into the United States from countries in which interest remained taxable.

As already noted, under a destination-basis consumption tax, MNCs would no longer have an incentive to shift income out of the United States at all, since the pricing of exports and imports would not affect a company's U.S. tax base. Those companies would have an incentive to distort transfer prices to shift income into the United States from countries that maintained business income taxes. The effects of such pressures on other countries are discussed further below.

Incentives would remain to use transfer prices to shift income out of the United States under an origin-basis consumption tax, since the prices of exports and imports would affect the U.S. tax base.

4

Net Capital Flows, Interest Rates, and the Capital Stock

N ow that we have seen what effect the introduction of a consumption tax would have on the location of tangible and intangible capital by multinational companies, we are in a position to take a broader look at the overall effect of consumption taxes on capital flows, interest rates, and the U.S. capital stock. This perspective requires looking at the behavior not only of multinational companies but also of other sectors, particularly those that are tax favored such as the state and local sector and owner-occupied housing. We must also distinguish between investment in debt and investment in equity, which are affected differently by a switch to a consumption tax. Focusing on debt is important too because some supporters of consumption taxes have claimed that such taxes would result in large declines in interest rates.[19]

Closed-Economy Effects

Before introducing trade and capital mobility, let us first consider a closed economy, because the case for a large drop in interest rates is weak even before bringing in capital mobility.

Let us also begin with only the business sector. As indicated earlier in the discussion of investment decisions by companies, the rate of return to equity investment should go up substantially. Companies would receive the equivalent of expensing on their investment in plant, equipment, and R&D because all business purchases are deductible, so companies will be able to offer higher rates of return on equity. In addition, shareholders will not be taxed on dividends.

The effect on interest rates is not so clear. From the business point of view, two offsetting forces affect the interest rates a company can offer. On the one hand, interest expenses are no longer deductible; interest is treated like equity. But companies can now expense their real investments. If expensing replaced economic depreciation, the loss in interest deductions would, in present-value terms, be about equivalent to the value of expensing. Accordingly, companies could offer the same interest rates as they did under the income tax.

But the process would not stop there. Companies would want to issue less debt and more equity because debt, with interest no longer being deductible, would not be as attractive as it was. This change, by itself, would tend to lower interest rates because fewer bonds would be available for purchase by shareholders. On the other hand, if the old interest rate is offered by companies, investors would reduce their demand for debt because the rate of return to equity has become much more attractive. This reduced demand for debt would, by itself, tend to raise the interest rates that companies have to offer. Putting these two forces together, we cannot firmly predict whether interest rates will fall or rise. In any case, a change in interest rates is likely to be small unless the increased after-tax return investors receive stimulates a great deal of additional saving.

Based on this analysis, we cannot predict a large fall in interest by pointing, as Hall and Rabushka did, to the interest rate differential between taxable and tax-exempt bonds. Exemption of interest income is only part of the story. The interest rates companies are able to offer and competition from equity, which would become much more attractive, must also be part of the analysis.

When nonbusiness sectors, such as housing and local governments, are reintroduced into the analysis, a fall in interest rates becomes more likely. Homeowners will find it more costly to invest in housing under a "pure" consumption tax because mortgage interest is no longer deductible. In addition, the consumption services provided by a house would presumably be taxed, like other consumption, albeit on the "prepayment" method because an investment in owner-occupied housing would not be deductible. Moreover, state and local governments would have to pay higher interest rates on their bonds because they would no longer have any advantage over other bonds, since all interest would be exempt from tax. Accordingly, prospective homeowners and state and local governments can be expected to borrow less under a consumption tax because they would no longer be "tax favored." The reduction in borrowing would tend to lower interest rates in the United States.

Open-Economy Effects

We now consider how trade and the mobility of capital alter the closed-economy analysis. As noted above, the rate of return to equity investment in the United States should go up substantially. Being able to expense new investments means companies would be able to offer shareholders the pretax rate of return. As a result, equity investment would flow into the United States. Foreign investors would increase their holdings of U.S. equity, and domestic companies and shareholders would shift more of their equity investments back to the United States.

But if there was any tendency for interest rates to fall, investment in debt would flow out of the United States. Both U.S. and foreign investors would find interest rates offered by issuers outside the United States relatively more attractive. Some of this foreign debt might even be de-nominated in dollars because a great deal of dollar debt is issued by governments and companies outside the United States. This competition from foreign interest rates would limit any tendency for U.S. interest rates to fall.

Because of the differing response of equity and debt investment, the *net* effect of international capital mobility on the U.S. capital stock is difficult to predict. If domestic saving is not very responsive to increasing rates of return, it is even conceivable that a consumption tax would lower the overall U.S. capital stock. Because debt is highly mo-bile internationally, and equity less so, the outflow of debt investment because of lower interest rates might outweigh the inflow of equity investment.

The effect of a consumption tax on different sectors is clearer. The U.S. business sector would unambiguously experience an inflow of capital. Because of the better treat-ment of corporate equity, corporations would enjoy a lower cost of capital, enabling them to expand their capital base. Any tendency for interest rates to fall would reinforce the expansion of capital in the business sector. But capital would flow out of the housing and state and local sectors. Homeowners would lose their mortgage interest deduc-tions, and the state and local sector would lose the advan-tage of tax-free debt. It may be that all the capital flowing out of these currently "tax-favored" sectors would not be absorbed by the business sector. In that case, there might be a net outflow of capital abroad in the form of shifts in the cross-border holdings of debt.

5

Simplicity and Compliance Issues

Replacing the current income tax with a consumption tax of the type considered here would yield significant benefits for the United States in terms of simplifying international tax rules and reducing compliance problems. Many of these benefits would stem from the consumption base of the taxes, which eliminates the need to define and measure foreign income. At the same time, old problems would remain in some cases, and some new problems would be created.

Benefits for the United States

Transfer Pricing. As already noted above, the need for the U.S. tax authorities to monitor transfer prices would disappear under a destination-basis consumption tax because transfer prices would no longer affect the U.S. tax base. This change would be a substantial benefit, since this area is one that currently creates substantial enforcement and compliance difficulties and burdens for MNCs and the U.S. tax authorities. The volume and variety of transactions between affiliates in MNC groups are high, and these transactions can involve the transfer of unique goods, services, or intangible assets that are difficult to value because there are no comparable transactions between unrelated parties. Of course, given that MNCs would have a strong incentive to shift income into the United States, a greater burden would be created for foreign tax authorities, and there could be more scope for disputes between them and MNCs.

Expense Allocation Rules. Because foreign income need not be measured, the tax code's source rules and the burdensome associated rules to allocate expenses between domestic and foreign income could be substantially simplified or would become unnecessary. Under an origin-basis consumption VAT or flat tax, expense allocation rules would be entirely irrelevant. All purchases by a U.S. business would be immediately deductible. Under a destination-basis consumption VAT, such as the USA business tax, the treatment of purchases would be the same, except that payments for imported goods, services, or intangible assets would effectively be nondeductible. Export sales would be exempt under a destination-basis tax, but all expenses would remain deductible to relieve the tax burden on all earlier stages of production. Under either of these forms of consumption tax, interest allocation rules would be unnecessary, since interest would not be deductible.

Foreign Tax Credits. The foreign tax credit rules provided under current law would become unnecessary under a consumption tax regime. These rules contain substantial complexity, including, for example, nine separate foreign tax credit baskets for different types of foreign income and look-through rules to retain the character of income as it passes through tiers of foreign subsidiaries. Foreign tax credit rules carry associated complications such as the need to determine the "earnings and profits" of foreign subsidiaries according to U.S. tax rules.

Passive Foreign Investment Rules. As a general rule, a U.S. shareholder in a foreign corporation, whether an individual or a company, pays no tax on the income earned by the foreign corporation until it is distributed. This arrangement creates an incentive for MNCs to avoid U.S. tax by having a foreign subsidiary in a low-tax jurisdiction hold passive investments. It creates an incentive for any U.S. taxpayer, corporate or individual, to hold passive investments in low-tax foreign jurisdictions through the vehicle of a foreign corporation. The tax code contains some fairly complicated rules that counteract this incentive by providing for current taxation of income from such investments.[20] A related compliance concern is that tax evaders may escape U.S. tax on investment income by keeping their money in secret accounts in tax havens, presenting a difficult enforcement challenge for the tax authorities. Since investment income is untaxed under a consumption tax, there would no longer be any tax motivation to keep passive investments abroad, and these rules and compliance concerns would be irrelevant.

Thin Capitalization and Interest Allocation. Interest deductibility under standard income tax systems creates the incentive for MNCs to arbitrage across countries with different tax rates by shifting their borrowing out of low-tax countries and into high-tax countries. The U.S. earnings-stripping and interest-allocation rules are designed to limit this kind of behavior. It would clearly be unnecessary under a consumption tax system in which interest is not deductible.[21]

Problems

Transfer Pricing. As noted previously, under an origin-basis consumption tax, incentives to distort transfer prices to shift income out of the United States would remain. The extent of the compliance problem would depend substantially on the rate of tax imposed. The problem would also be exacerbated, however, by the absence of some of the backstops to the transfer-pricing rules currently built into our international tax rules. These backstops include the taxation of worldwide income (albeit often only on a deferred basis) and the current taxation of passive income and foreign base company sales income under subpart F of the tax code.

Reclassifying Sales Receipts as Interest. Because of the dichotomy between real and financial transactions, R-based consumption taxes such as the flat tax and the USA business tax create an incentive to reclassify part of the taxable sales price of a good sold to consumers as nontaxable interest on an installment sale. In an open economy, this incentive also exists under an origin-basis tax for sales to foreigners in an income tax country because only the sales component would be taxable in the United States but the foreigner can deduct both sales and interest components. Similarly, the incentive exists under an origin-basis tax to overstate the purchase price component of imports and understate the interest component. Note that this is essentially a variant of the transfer-pricing problem, but these transactions need not be with related parties. The potentially large magnitude of trade payables and receivables could make this problem significant.

Taxable Imports and Exempt Exports. The experience of countries that impose VATs shows that application of a destination-basis consumption tax can create compliance problems and complexities because of the need to distinguish between deductible domestic purchases and effectively nondeductible imports and between taxable domestic sales and exempt exports. The extent of these problems depends on the controls at the border, the type of consumption tax (subtraction method versus invoice-credit method), and the type of imports or exports (merchandise or services).

The problem for imports is reduced if the credit-invoice method is used, since a company would presumably get a credit for taxes on its purchases only if it can show that those taxes have actually been paid, either at the border on imports or at an earlier stage of domestic production. Under the subtraction method, the problem for merchandise imports is also much reduced if, as in the USA business tax, there is a tax at the border, because then the importing business does not have to distinguish between deductible and nondeductible expenses. But if under a subtraction-method tax there is no tax at the border, the problem can be substantial because a company must distinguish between domestic purchases and imports—only the former are deductible—even though the goods may be identical.

Although it is relatively straightforward to impose a tax on merchandise imports, it is not so easy in the case of imported services. For example, no border controls could be used to impose a tax on foreign advertising or consulting services that might be transmitted electronically over a satellite. This problem could be ameliorated if for expenses to be deductible they had to have been paid to a seller that provided a taxpayer identification number. Even in this case, tax auditors might have to examine a chain of transactions.

An additional level of complexity would be added in cases in which a service was provided partly domestically and partly from abroad. For example, an international consulting firm might prepare a report to which both its New York and its London offices had contributed. The fee for this report would need to be divided into separate components representing compensation for the services performed by the two different offices. In principle, this division does not affect the total tax base, as long as the component that does not bear an import tax is included in the receipts of the New York office for U.S. tax purposes. Additional difficulties with respect to financial services provided by financial intermediaries are discussed below.

Consumers would also have the incentive to use foreign services, such as credit-card processing. Cross-border shopping could be an issue as well. International mail order for merchandise would not seem to create a new problem as long as customs duties are imposed on packages, as under the current system.

Moreover, compliance problems would arise in distinguishing exports from domestic sales. Goods could be shipped from one U.S. port and landed in another. Problems of this kind have been encountered in the case of ozone-depleting chemicals, whose domestic use is subject to a high tax under current law.

These problems could be severe if a destination-basis VAT were imposed at a very high rate, such as would be required to replace the income tax entirely. If the states followed suit and replaced their sales taxes with a VAT modeled after the federal VAT, the combined tax rate would likely be very high in comparison with other VAT countries.

Financial Intermediaries. The familiar problem of financial intermediaries in R-based consumption tax schemes, such as a VAT, arises because of the difference in the treatment between real and financial transactions. Interest payments and receipts are ignored. Therefore, services provided in exchange for interest rate spreads— for example, transactions services to consumers instead of higher interest rates on their checking account balances—are not subject to tax.

This problem would seem to exist only for services to consumers. If untaxed financial services are provided to a business, it gets no deduction (or credit) but has to pay tax on the final sale. The same is true for loan expenses incurred by a bank on its business loans. Tax will be paid on the full gross product of the loan at the business (borrower) level. With equal tax rates for all business taxpayers, the failure to impute income to one of the stages is offset by the absence of a deduction at the next stage. In addition, some financial services, such as investment management, are often investment rather than consumption. These services are provided with the object of producing a higher return from the investor's capital. The value of the goods or services produced with that capital is taxed. In these cases, all the proper tax can be collected when the goods and services are sold to consumers, and the imputation of interest spreads on loans proposed by Hall and Rabushka (1995) seems largely unnecessary.[22]

International transactions would not seem to exacerbate the problem of untaxed financial services to a great extent. Under the destination basis, service exports would be exempt, and service imports by business would be nondeductible anyway. The problem in this case would be largely limited to the direct import of services by consumers. Under the origin basis, the distortions created might be greater, since service exports should be taxed and imports deducted; however, the direct import of services by consumers would no longer be an issue, since such services should be untaxed in any case.

If it is deemed necessary to impute service fees to the transactions of financial intermediaries, then international transactions will add some complexity. It will be difficult to determine the appropriate allocation of imputed fees to foreign customers.

Consumption Abroad. Because the base of a destination-basis consumption tax is consumption in the United States in each period, it can create an incentive for residents to avoid the tax by consuming abroad. One way to do this is through vacationing abroad. Perhaps more important, a retiree might avoid the tax by emigrating to a country that imposed a lower consumption tax, or no consumption tax at all. Under a destination-basis tax, the tax saving from emigration would show itself through the tax-induced difference between the U.S. and foreign price levels. Under a personal consumption tax such as the USA individual tax, a U.S. taxpayer could benefit from the deduction for savings while accumulating wealth and then avoid tax when subsequently dissaving by emigrating.[23]

The incentive to emigrate would not exist under an origin-basis tax such as the flat tax. There would be no tax-induced difference between the foreign and the domestic price levels. In real terms, the tax on any income earned in the United States is not rebated at the border when it is used to finance foreign consumption, as it is under a destination-basis consumption tax.

6
Transition Incidence

S ome of the more problematic issues associated with adoption of a consumption tax relate to transition effects.[24] In a closed economy, perhaps the major consequence of the transition is that, in the absence of transition rules,[25] imposition of a consumption tax effectively imposes a one-time tax on the existing stock of wealth in the economy.[26] In general terms, with the transition the existing stock of wealth is taxed when it is consumed. In an open economy, an additional issue is the distribution of transition effects between foreign and U.S. investors. In particular, the issue is to what extent foreign investors in U.S. assets and U.S. investors in foreign assets bear the transition tax. It turns out that the distinction between origin and destination bases is crucial. To simplify the analysis, we examine the international transition effects of introducing a consumption tax while largely ignoring the effects of eliminating the income tax.

We start by considering 100 percent equity ownership of a U.S. asset existing at the time the consumption tax is introduced. Introduction of a flat-rate consumption tax involves taxing at a given rate all the future cash flow from the asset, if the cash flow is used to finance consumption in the United States. Now consider the effect on a foreign holder of that equity interest if the consumption tax is imposed on the destination basis. In this case, the purchasing power in terms of U.S. consumption of the stream of cash flow from that equity interest will have fallen in proportion to the tax rate at the business level. But recall that the real return to a U.S. investment is effectively paid out to foreigners in U.S. exports, so the tax on that return is rebated at the border. Therefore, the real value to the foreign investor of the cash flow from the U.S. equity interest will not change, and the foreign investor escapes any transition burden from the introduction of a destination-basis consumption tax. On the most basic level, a destination-basis consumption tax falls on domestic consumption in each period, so it should not be a surprise that a foreign investor escapes the burden of the tax.

Now turn to the transition effect of imposing a destination-basis tax on a U.S. owner of a foreign asset. Recall that the real return to the U.S. owner of a foreign asset is paid out in imports to the United States, and those imports are taxed under the destination basis. Therefore, the U.S. owner of the foreign asset bears the transition impact of the tax in full, as long as he continues to consume in the United States.

Consider next an origin-basis consumption tax. In this case, the exports that represent the real return to the foreign owner of U.S. assets receive no rebate of tax under the origin basis, and the imports that represent the real return of the U.S. owner of foreign assets are not taxed. Therefore, in contrast to the case of a destination-basis tax, the foreign equity holder bears the transition burden in the same way as any domestic equity holder would, while a U.S. owner of foreign assets escapes the transition impact altogether.

One conclusion from this analysis is that an origin-basis consumption tax could be expected to impose more of its transition burden on foreigners, to the extent that transition rules do not otherwise affect the burden. This feature may be viewed as attractive to the extent that it represents a lump-sum transfer from foreigners to the

United States. Given that the U.S. net foreign asset position is currently negative, the United States would gain more from the transition tax on the U.S. assets of foreigners than it would lose in the transition tax on foreign assets held by U.S. residents.

By focusing on the transition effect on equity holders, we have ignored the effects on debt. In general, the analysis of those effects will be little different from the closed-economy analysis in which the distribution of transition losses between debt and equity holders depends largely on the price-level adjustment that occurs with the transition and the terms of outstanding debt contracts (for example, whether bonds are indexed).

7
Reaction of Other Countries

I n the discussion so far, we have only touched on the effects of a U.S. policy change of this nature on other countries and what their responses might be. In fact, other countries might well react to the extent that the U.S. policy change threatened to cause significant capital flows to the United States at their expense and to erode their tax bases through MNCs' shifting debt from their U.S. books and, under a destination-basis tax, transfer-pricing profits into the United States.

Other countries might move to protect their tax bases from the effects of MNC debt shifting by instituting rules to limit interest deductions, such as thin capitalization rules and rules to allocate interest deductions among the members of an MNC group. Such a reaction would have a direct effect on the United States only to the extent that policies were targeted specifically at U.S. MNCs.

Other countries might also take measures to extend their tax reach to encompass income that the United States no longer taxes. This could be done through changes to income source rules, expense allocation rules, and accrual taxation of foreign income. If the United States moved to a destination-basis consumption tax, foreign tax authorities might also respond by taking more aggressive positions on transfer pricing between the United States and MNC affiliates located in their country. The standard mechanism for dealing with such cases provided in bilateral treaties for eliminating double taxation might be difficult to use to resolve such cases, because the U.S. tax base would be unaffected by any changes to transfer prices imposed by a foreign tax authority.

Other countries might also feel pressure to reduce their taxes on capital income. This pressure would come both from the shifting of debt from the United States to those countries and from the likely flows of equity investment from those countries to the United States. The ultimate result could be lower taxes on capital income worldwide, and, consequently, the effects on capital flows to the United States that were posited above would be muted.

Whether the total effect of these changes would push the global economy toward or away from efficiency is unclear. A uniformly lower level of capital income taxes would likely lead to fewer distortions in the allocation of capital across countries and a globally increased return to saving. To replace lost revenue from capital income taxes, however, governments are likely to have to raise other taxes, in particular, taxes on labor income, either directly or, following the U.S. lead, through increased reliance on consumption taxes.

Tax Treaties and Withholding Taxes

The analysis to this point has not yet dealt with the implications of moving to a consumption tax system for our network of tax treaties. The United States currently has bilateral tax treaties with over forty countries. These treaties provide substantial benefits to cross-border investment by, among other things, lowering withholding tax rates on cross-border income flows, scaling back the tax reach of host countries, and preventing discriminatory treatment of foreign investment by host countries. Most provisions of these treaties apply only to taxes on income, and the

United States would be unilaterally eliminating its income tax. The question arises whether other countries would perceive themselves as unilaterally providing benefits to U.S. investors and receiving little in return under their treaties. In that case, foreign countries might be tempted to terminate their treaties with the United States.

It turns out that U.S. tax treaty partners would face conflicting incentives in this regard, so that the outcome for U.S. treaties is unclear. On one side, other countries might wish to dispense with the constraints on their tax reach imposed by a tax treaty so that they can extend their tax reach further to tax income that the United States no longer taxes and thereby reduce the incentive for their companies to invest in the United States. But there would also be potential benefits to maintaining a tax treaty with the United States.

If the United States maintained its withholding taxes on income payments to foreigners, those taxes could provide a disincentive for U.S. tax treaty partners to terminate their treaties. Under current law, the United States imposes a 30 percent withholding tax on payments of dividends, interest (other than portfolio interest, which is exempt), and royalties to foreigners. These rates are generally substantially reduced under tax treaties, sometimes to zero for direct-investment interest and royalties and 5 percent for direct-investment dividends. If the United States retained its statutory withholding taxes, treaty partners with significant investment in the United States would stand to lose at the least the substantial benefit of the treaty withholding rate reductions. They might lose even more because of the nondiscrimination provision of these treaties. Under this provision, a treaty partner is not permitted to impose a greater tax burden on the resident individuals or companies of the other country than it imposes on its own residents. Although withholding taxes on cross-border payments fall only on foreigners, they are not considered to violate the nondiscrimination article because they are deemed to be imposed in lieu of the income tax on resident recipients of such payments. Since under the consumption tax plans no tax is generally imposed on resident recipients, the withholding taxes might be viewed as violating the discrimination article.[27] In this case, residents of treaty partners would face no withholding tax at all if the treaty were retained but a 30 percent tax if it were terminated.[28]

U.S. tax treaty partners might also be deterred from terminating their tax treaties because they might not wish their higher statutory withholding tax rates to apply to U.S. investors. They might be concerned that this would make their country an even less competitive location for U.S. investment, particularly since the United States would no longer provide a foreign tax credit.

8
Conclusions

Our objective in this volume has been to show that international considerations can be important in evaluating the effects of any radical tax reform that involves replacing our income tax system with a consumption tax. Open-economy effects can alter outcomes that would be anticipated in a closed-economy setting. We saw that investment in the U.S. business sector would become more attractive and that there would likely be increases in investment in the United States by U.S. and foreign MNCs. But at the same time, the total U.S. capital stock could actually fall, because while equity capital would flow into the U.S. business sector, debt capital might flow out of the United States. U.S. multinational companies might also have a greater incentive to use their technology and know-how in the United States, but it is unclear on balance whether they would do more of their R&D at home or abroad.

International considerations also raise new issues. A consumption tax would permit substantial simplification of complicated international tax rules and would eliminate certain compliance problems. But there would also be new administrative and compliance issues. The choice between origin and destination bases for the treatment of exports and imports turns out to have important consequences in this regard. A destination-basis tax eliminates the transfer-pricing problem, but it creates incentives for cross-border shopping and consumption abroad. An origin-basis tax does not give rise to incentives for consumption abroad or cross-border shopping, but the transfer-pricing problem remains.

Finally, the reactions of other countries need to be taken into account. The elimination of taxes on capital income by the United States would likely lead to heightened competition for capital and tax base. Other countries would come under pressure to protect their tax base by taxing at least some of the tax base vacated by the United States. Ultimately, other countries would probably be forced to lower the level of their taxation of capital income as well.

Notes

1. Merrill, Wertz, and Shah (1995) find that tax revenues from nonfinancial corporations would rise under the USA business tax and the Armey flat tax at plausible tax rates. Their analysis, however, reveals nothing about the total tax burden on capital income. Their comparison ignores the taxation of capital income at the personal level under the current tax system. They also attribute taxes on wages to the corporate tax burden under the USA business tax but not under the current tax system or the flat tax.

2. See Institute for Fiscal Studies (1978).

3. Since interest income and interest expense are ignored, financial intermediaries will have a negative tax base because of their purchase of goods and services from other firms. The implications are discussed later in this volume.

4. Note that the treatment of interest under the R and $(R+F)$ bases is essentially equivalent. Since the present value of interest and principal repayments on a loan is equal to the amount of the loan, the deductions and inclusions for debt under the $(R+F)$ base are equivalent to ignoring debt transactions under the R base.

5. The expected present value of rental payments for the use of property over the life of the property should be equal to the market value of the property. Since under current tax rules, proceeds from the sale of property by U.S. residents are generally treated as U.S.-source income, neutrality in tax treatment would require rental receipts to be treated as U.S.-source income as well.

6. The proposals themselves are vague on this point. The USA proposal appears to include royalty receipts in the base but does not mention royalty payments in the context of deductions, nor does it discuss their treatment under the destination basis. The Armey proposal appears to be completely silent on the subject of royalties.

7. This reflects the fact that there are restrictions on the extent to which MNCs can treat contributions of capital to a foreign subsidiary as debt, and the bulk of U.S. direct investment abroad and foreign direct investment in the United States is in fact characterized as equity. Although direct investment may also be financed partly with local debt, our subsequent discussion of interest rate effects indicates that taking local debt finance into account would only reinforce the conclusions drawn here.

8. Hartman (1985) has shown that deferral can be equivalent to exemption in its effects when foreign investment is financed out of a subsidiary's retained earnings. Furthermore, the ability to cross-credit, so that excess credits from high-tax foreign income can be used to offset U.S. tax on low-tax foreign income, also can push the system toward an exemption system in its effects. Where a U.S. MNC has excess foreign tax credits overall, there is effectively no U.S. tax on additional income from a low-tax foreign source. Based on calculations using 1990 data, Grubert and Mutti (1995) show that the average effective U.S. tax rate on the foreign income of U.S. MNCs from active investments is remarkably low, about 2 percent when calculated using a standard definition of foreign income and negative if foreign income is defined to exclude royalty receipts.

9. Viewed in real terms, the stream of imports representing the real return to the investment would be taxed.

10. These countries include Canada, France, Germany, and the Netherlands.

11. As in the case of Japan and the United Kingdom.

12. McLure and Zodrow (1994) present this argument.

13. Of course, the application of transfer-pricing rules is unlikely to be perfect, and the opportunity to shift above-normal returns to low-tax jurisdictions will create incentives to locate some investment in those jurisdictions.

14. It is possible that a consumption tax would be implemented in which the treatment of royalties was inconsistent with the general destination- or origin-basis treatment of exports and imports of goods and services. If receipts of royalties from abroad were taxed under a generally destination-basis tax, it would be the equivalent of a double tax on the income from the intangible because the imports financed by the income flow from abroad are taxed as well. If royalties from abroad were exempt under a generally origin-basis tax, the income from the intangible would be consumed effectively free of U.S. tax because the imports represented by that income flow are not taxed.

15. Marketing activities can also create intangible assets, but

there may be less flexibility in location choice since these activities are frequently market specific.

16. There might, however, be indirect effects. For example, since all investment would be expensed, R&D and advertising would no longer be favored relative to investment in tangible capital.

17. This is likely also to be true for an $(R+F)$-based tax such as the McLure and Zodrow (1995) proposal. As explained above, the inclusion of new borrowing and deduction for payments of interest and principal is equivalent to the nondeductibility of interest under the R base.

18. See Altshuler and Mintz (1994) and Froot and Hines (1995).

19. See Hall and Rabushka (1995).

20. These are the passive foreign investment company rules and parts of the subpart F rules.

21. As noted previously, $(R+F)$-based consumption taxes do provide for interest deductibility, but since new borrowing is included in the tax base and repayments of debt deducted, the treatment of debt is equivalent in present-value terms to interest nondeductibility.

22. See Grubert and Mackie (1996) for an extensive treatment of these issues.

23. The USA individual tax reduces this incentive to some extent by taxing citizens and green card holders on their dissaving even if they no longer reside in the United States and by continuing to tax former citizens and green card holders under some circumstances.

24. See Sarkar and Zodrow (1993) for a review of some of the major transition problems.

25. The USA tax proposal contains transition rules to ameliorate this impact, but they add considerable complexity. In addition, estimates of large increases in savings from moving to a consumption tax are generally predicated on the lack of any transition rules. See, for example, Auerbach and Kotlikoff (1987).

26. This transition impact could be moderated to the extent that the elimination of income taxes increased the after-tax yield to wealth holders. In this case, the initial transition losses in wealth are offset to a greater extent the longer the wealth holder can take advantage of the higher after-tax yields, that is, the longer the period before the wealth is consumed. This moderating influence, however, may be diminished by international capital flows, since any rise in domestic after-tax yields would be moderated by an inflow of foreign capital.

27. The USA individual tax might be an exception, since receipts of dividends and interest are included in the tax base.

28. As Avi-Yonah (1996) has pointed out, another country might actually wish to see the United States impose withholding taxes to discourage outflows of capital to the United States. But an offsetting consideration is that that country's MNCs would then face a tax disadvantage in the United States relative to domestic U.S. companies or MNCs from other countries that maintained their treaties with the United States.

Bibliography

Alliance USA. "Description and Explanation of the Unlimited Savings Allowance Income Tax System." *Tax Notes* 66, no. 11 (March 10, 1995): 1483–1575.

Altshuler, Rosanne, and Jack Mintz. "U.S. Interest Allocation Rules: Effects and Policy." NBER Working Paper no. 4712. Cambridge, Mass.: National Bureau of Economic Research, 1994.

Auerbach, Alan J., and Laurence J. Kotlikoff. *Dynamic Fiscal Policy*. Cambridge, U.K.: Cambridge University Press, 1987.

Avi-Yonah. "Comment on Grubert and Newlon. "The International Implications of Consumption Tax Proposals."" *National Tax Journal* 49, no. 2 (June 1996): 259–65.

Baxter, Marianne, and Mario Crucini. "Explaining Saving-Investment Correlations." *American Economic Review* 83, no. 3 (June 1993): 416–36.

Bradford, David F. *Untangling the Income Tax*. Cambridge, Mass.: Harvard University Press, 1986.

Dixit, Avinash. "Tax Policy in Open Economies." In *Handbook of Public Economics*, ed. A. Auerbach and M. Feldstein. Amsterdam: North-Holland, 1985.

Feldstein, Martin S., and Charles Y. Horioka. "Domestic Savings and International Capital Flows." *Economic Journal* 90 (June 1980): 314–29.

Feldstein, Martin, and Paul Krugman. "International Trade Effects of Value-added Taxation." In *Taxation in the Global Economy*, ed. A. Razin and J. Slemrod. Chicago: University of Chicago Press, 1990.

Frankel, Jeffrey A. "Quantifying International Capital Mobility in the 1980s." In *National Saving and Economic Performance*, ed. D. Bernheim and J. Shoven. Chicago: University of Chicago Press, 1991.

French, Kenneth R., and James M. Poterba. "Investor Diversification and International Equity Markets." NBER Working Paper no. 3609. Cambridge, Mass.: National Bureau of Economic Research, 1991.

Froot, Kenneth A., and James R. Hines, Jr. "Interest Allocation Rules, Financing Patterns, and the Operations of U.S. Multinationals." In *The Effects of Taxation on Multinational Corporations*, ed. M. Feldstein, J. R. Hines, Jr., and R. G. Hubbard. Chicago: University of Chicago Press, 1995.

Gordon, Roger H. "Can Capital Income Taxes Survive in Open Economies?" *Journal of Finance* 47, no. 3 (July 1992): 1159–80.

Gordon, Roger H., and Joel Slemrod. "Do We Collect Any Revenue from Taxing Capital Income?" In *Tax Policy and the Economy*, vol. 2, ed. L. Summers. Cambridge, Mass: MIT Press, 1988.

Goulder, Lawrence H., John B. Shoven, and John Whalley. "Domestic Tax Policy and the Foreign Sector: The Importance of Alternative Foreign Sector Formulations to Results from a General Equilibrium Tax Analysis Model." In *Behavioral Simulation Methods in Tax Policy Analysis*, ed. M. Feldstein. Chicago: University of Chicago Press, 1983.

Grossman, Gene M. "Border Tax Adjustments: Do They Distort Trade?" *Journal of International Economics* 10 (1980): 117–28.

Grubert, Harry, and James Mackie. "An Unnecessary Complication: Must Financial Services Be Taxed under a Consumption Tax?" U.S. Treasury Department, Office of Tax Analysis, August 1996.

Grubert, Harry, and John Mutti. "International Aspects of Corporate Tax Integration: The Contrasting Role of Debt and Equity Flows." *National Tax Journal* 47, no. 1 (March 1994): 111–33.

————. "Taxing Multinationals in a World with Portfolio Flows and R&D: Is Capital Export Neutrality Obsolete?" *International Tax and Public Finance*, no. 2 (1995): 439–57.

Grubert, Harry, and T. Scott Newlon. "The International Implications of Consumption Tax Proposals." *National Tax Journal* 48, no. 4. (December 1995): 619–47.

Hall, Robert E., and Alvin Rabushka. *The Flat Tax*. Stanford: Hoover Institution Press, 1st ed. 1985, 2d ed. 1995.

————. *Low Tax, Simple Tax, Flat Tax*. New York: McGraw-Hill, 1983.

Hartman, David. "Tax Policy and Foreign Direct Investment." *Journal of Public Economics* 26 (1985): 107–21.

Huizinga, Harry. "The Incidence of Interest Withholding Taxes: Evidence from the LDC Loan Market." *Journal of Public Economics* (forthcoming).

Institute for Fiscal Studies. *The Structure and Reform of Direct Taxation* (Meade committee report). London: Allen and Unwin, 1978.

McLure, Charles E., and George R. Zodrow. "Creditability of the Cash Flow Tax." Unpublished submission to the Treasury Department, October, 1994.

————. "A Hybrid Approach to the Direct Taxation of Consumption." Proceedings of a conference sponsored by the Hoover Institution, Washington, D.C., May 11, 1995.

Merrill, Peter, Ken Wertz, and Shvetank Shah. "Corporate Tax Liability under the USA and Flat Taxes." *Tax Notes* 68, no. 6 (August 7, 1995): 741–45.

Mintz, Jack M., and Jesus Seade. "Cash Flow or Income? The Choice of Base for Company Taxation." Policy

Planning and Research Working Paper no. 177. Washington, D.C.: World Bank, April 1989.

Sarkar, Shounak, and George R. Zodrow. "Transitional Issues in Moving to a Direct Consumption Tax." *National Tax Journal* 46, no. 3 (September 1993): 359–76.

About the Authors

HARRY GRUBERT is an international economist in the Office of Tax Analysis of the U.S. Department of the Treasury. He has also worked in the Labor Department and the Office of Management and Budget. He has published a number of papers on the international aspects of tax policy. He received his Ph.D. from the Massachusetts Institute of Technology.

T. SCOTT NEWLON is an economist in the Office of Tax Analysis of the U.S. Department of the Treasury, where he works on a variety of international tax policy issues. He has published a number of papers on international tax subjects. He received his Ph.D. from Princeton University.

AEI STUDIES ON TAX REFORM
R. Glenn Hubbard and Diana Furchtgott-Roth
Series Editors